Harvesting H2o

A prepper's guide to the collection, treatment, and storage of drinking water while living off the grid.

Nicholas Hyde

ISBN-13: 978-1481269933

ISBN-10: 1481269933

Table of Contents

Introduction

The provision of safe drinking water is always the first order of business in any survival situation. If you have seen survivalist Bear Grylls skydive into remote backcountry areas on his cable TV show, you know that locating fresh water is the first thing he always does. While the human body can survive for a month or more without food, it cannot go more than a few days without water. In extremely hot climates, you could be dead in a matter of hours.

It logically follows that as a prepper or an off-grid homesteader, your first priority is maintaining a sustainable potable water source. It is not practical to attempt to simply store a large supply beforehand, because we humans just consume it too quickly. Even if you have the equivalent of an Olympic-size swimming pool at your disposal, your family will go through it all within a few short years. You need a renewable source of fresh water, and you need a reliable system of making it safe for human consumption. That's what this book is about.

In the following pages, we will discuss in considerable detail the best methods of harvesting, keeping, and purifying fresh water for human consumption. Fortunately, this can be accomplished without sacrificing the comforts of a modern home, if you so choose. Producing your own delicious drinking water is a very satisfying project, and there will be no public utility water bill to pay.

One thing we have going for us is water is never very far away. More than 2/3 of the earth is covered with it, which seems appropriate, being as the human body consists of roughly 2/3 water. However, only 3% of the water on earth is fresh water. (Living in modern times does have its advantages; saltwater can now be quickly converted into fresh drinking water using convenient equipment which is affordable to most homesteaders, and we will cover that.) Of the earth's fresh water supply, nearly 70% is frozen or trapped inside of glaciers. The overwhelming majority of the rest of it lies underground, leaving less than 1% on the surface in streams, lakes, ponds, and swamps.

There's more. As you know, water comes in three different physical forms. The earth's atmosphere contains another large supply of it in gas form, perhaps enough to fill all of the earth's rivers to their high water mark and then some.

It's a good thing the earth yields such an abundant supply, because people consume an awful lot of H2o. In America alone, it has been estimated that more than 390 billion (with a b) gallons of water are used every single day. Each time a person flushes a toilet, between 1.5 and 5 gallons are used, depending on the age and efficiency of the toilet. Turning the water off while you brush your teeth actually saves several gallons. If your toilet runs, it is likely that 10+ gallons are wasted before you remember to go in and jiggle the handle. This is the reason many off-grid homes are being built which use non-potable, recycled water (grey water) for toilets, irrigation, and even in some appliances such as washing machines.

When a person chooses to move to an off-the-grid lifestyle, conservation usually becomes a major motivating force. One is suddenly more aware of one's own wasteful, modern living habits, and begins to make compensating adjustments. Water is the most precious resource, so it is usually the biggest conservation target. Of course, this depends greatly on where you live. If your home is in the Pacific Northwest or Great Britain, there is always plenty more water on the way – usually within a matter of days, at the longest – so the only concern is how to best collect it, treat it, and store it.

The rest of us will need to pay attention to our supply and stop living like a blissfully blind city-slicker (the water system in New York City leaks more than 35 million gallons a day). That doesn't mean you can't take a shower every day. It does mean you need to pay attention to your consumption habits and make an effort not to squander your resources needlessly. However, in no way should you feel compelled to reduce your own personal consumption of fresh water! Quite the contrary; you should enjoy it all the more when you harvest it yourself and cease to spill so much of it down the drains. Properly supplied, you will not be able to drink your way into a personal drought, so by all means have those 8 glasses a day, and make all the homebrew you want. You may, however, want to think twice about washing your car with potable water every weekend.

In ancient times, thousands of years before residential plumbing, people still had enough water to drink. If they could do it, you certainly can. Back then, they didn't know about germs. Consequently, health problems ran rampant through societies and life expectancies were relatively short. These days, you can have the best of both worlds. You can enjoy the simple pleasure of harvesting drinking water from nature, and make it safe to drink, too. Since that is by far the most important step, let's start there...

Harvesting H2o

The Dangers of Drinking Wild Water

Although fresh water supplies can be found almost anywhere there is land, it is estimated that around 90% of the earth's surface water is contaminated and unsafe to drink as-is. Exactly how unsafe ranges from the presence of minor microorganisms which may cause a mild upset stomach to harboring dangerous bacteria or virus strains which will result in violent illness, disease, and even death.

Before Louis Pasteur discovered germs in the mid 1800's, it was common practice in many societies not to even consume water. Back in those days, people would drink beer, wine, or various forms of tea instead. Water from the surface of the earth was known to be risky and unsafe, although they didn't know why. What they did know was that once water was processed into beverages, it was safe. So, that is what they drank. Fermented juices were typically diluted with water to create weak alcoholic beverages which could be consumed without making one too intoxicated to work. This is a practice that goes back to ancient times. The Hebrews of Biblical times would dilute wine with water, about three parts water to one part wine, for regular daily consumption with meals. That was enough alcohol to sanitize the water being consumed, for their purposes.

Well-water is much safer than surface water as a general rule, but only once you know the well is safe. In the old days, the household servants would be the guinea pigs for newly dug wells. If they didn't get sick, then the land owners would know it was safe to drink from, at least for a while. It is possible for a good well to become contaminated from surface water and go bad. Springs are known to be a reasonably safe bet for good drinking water, but only at the source, where the water first emerges from underground. After it has run along the surface for a while, it becomes contaminated. Likewise, rainwater is safe to drink before it comes into contact with anything. The process of vaporization purifies it, so when it reforms as a liquid it is about as pure as it gets (yes, even "acid rain").

Whenever you see a national disaster in a third world country reported on the news, one of the main concerns is a cholera outbreak. This happens because wastewater drainage systems become rerouted and find their way into drinking water supplies, contaminating them. It doesn't usually happen right away, as the bacteria require time to colonize. In places like Zimbabwe, residents don't have access to chemical treatments, such as chlorine, so it is easy for drinking water reservoirs to become spoiled. One small infection will eventually spread through the entire supply. After the Haiti earthquake in 2010, a severe cholera outbreak occurred one full year later. Cholera typically has about a 1% fatality rate.

Roughly 4% of all human illness is attributed to waterborne disease, estimated to be responsible for nearly two million deaths annually. According to the World Health Organization, almost 90% of waterborne disease cases are simply the result of unsanitary practices with unsafe water supplies. These figures do not include mosquito-spread diseases such as malaria. (Mosquitos require a water source in order to proliferate, but their usage of the water supply is not known to directly cause it to become unsafe for human consumption.)

The culprits are microorganisms who make their home in fresh water. They fall into four broad categories: bacteria, parasites, protozoa, and viruses. The old adage that running water is safe to drink while standing water is unsafe is a misnomer; while you are less likely to encounter protozoa and bacteria in running water, parasites and viruses are not deterred by it.

Bacterial infections in drinking water are the most common and the most feared. Bacteria can be found everywhere on our planet and some dangerous strains do make their homes in surface freshwater supplies, especially those located in warmer climates. An example would be Legionella, which is responsible for Legionnaires' disease. However, most bacteria contaminations in drinking water supplies are introduced by an outside source, such as sewage, which the bacteria use to culture up and become strong enough to result in a major infection. Waterborne diseases in this category include botulism, cholera, e.coli, dysentery, salmonella, and typhoid.

Parasites in drinking water are essentially very small animals, usually ingested by people in egg or larvae form. Once they get into your digestive tract, the eggs hatch and these animals are then capable of traveling through the walls of the digestive tract and taking up residence in human tissue or the bloodstream. If these creatures are living in the water supply, it has become contaminated and anyone consuming that water without properly sanitizing it first is liable to infection. This category of waterborne diseases includes blood flukes and worms such as tapeworm. The record tapeworm pulled out of a human was 37 feet long.

Protozoa are categorized as plant life and include algae, fungus, and amoeba. A drinking water source that acquires protozoan contamination is usually the result of coming into contact with sewage or animal waste. However, some protozoan infections have been detected naturally in groundwater, and are therefore the primary risk of well water contamination. Typical signs of infection in humans include flu-like symptoms, abdominal pain, and diarrhea.

Viruses are prevalent on planet earth, and unfortunately some of the more dangerous varieties will readily take up residence in drinking water supplies which have not been properly treated. We all know what the symptoms of a virus feel like. Waterborne viruses can be deadly and include Hepatitis A, SARS, and Polio.

Keep in mind, contaminated water can infect your body even if you don't drink it. All it has to do is come into contact with something that you do ingest, such as food plates, silverware, drinking vessels, your toothbrush, the little cup you use for toothbrush water, or even just washing your hands and face with it. This is especially true with bacterial and viral infections. It is important to clean your eating and drinking utensils with purified water only, and only use purified water for personal hygiene purposes, including washing your face and hands.

By now, you should have a better understanding of the dangers of drinking untreated wild water, even if it comes from a well (especially a shallow or unsealed well) or a spring. Unless you are collecting rainwater via a sanitized container and consuming it immediately, freshwater cannot be considered safe for consumption until it has been tested or treated and stored in sanitary tanks. Fortunately, purifying your off-grid drinking water supply is a fairly easy thing to do at home.

Harvesting H2o

Purifying Water at Home

There are three basic methods of making fresh water safe for human consumption: Heat, Chemical Treatment, and Filtering. Which method you should use (including potentially combining methods), depends on the clarity and quality of the water you are harvesting, and practicality considerations based on your situation. Most homesteaders simply pump filtered deep-well water into their home via an electric-powered pump, and this does the job nicely in most areas.

My family has a fishing cabin in Montana. The well water in Montana is some of the most wonderful-tasting stuff I have ever had the pleasure of drinking. It is known to be safe straight from the well in that region, but homebuilders these days will usually put a filtration system in place, usually in the homes themselves, under the sinks. The refrigerator we have there dispenses water and ice and includes a filter in the water line. As mentioned in the last chapter, the main concern with well water is protozoa, which modern water filters effectively remove.

Commercially-dug wells are deep, usually a couple hundred feet or more depending on the geology of your area. Septic tanks are always placed on a downslope from the house and well, in an effort to keep heavy rains and mild floods from allowing the septic tank contents to contaminate the water supply. This is what happens (on a larger scale) when there are natural disasters in underdeveloped areas. Normally, it's not much of a concern for homesteaders, as septic tanks are sealed from above, as are wells. The ground is a natural filter, and quite effective. Septic tanks are buried just beneath the surface, so there is usually a large layer of earth separating it from the groundwater. This is also why you don't need to worry about being downhill from a neighbor's septic tank, assuming some discernible acreage lies between you.

Rain barrels (and the like) are quite another matter. In order to collect rain in a barrel, it must come into contact with contaminated surfaces. Many rain barrel systems collect water off of rooftops via rain gutters. This is obviously dirty water by the time it is gathered in the barrel, often containing large debris such as leaves, dirt, and even pieces of rusty metal broken off from the rain gutter. As it is stored, it only gets worse, being a prime breeding ground for bacterial infections. Water harvested in this manner is normally only used for irrigation purposes. It can be made reasonably safe for drinking if need be, but the process is more involved than simply filtering it.

Purifying dirty water, such as that from rain barrels or muddy standing water, can be done in a three-step process. The first step is to use a coarse filter to remove all large, visible matter from the water and give it a degree of clarity. We have seen Bear Grylls do this on television using his shirt as a water filter. I even saw one episode where he was in the

Utah desert filling his canteen with water dripping from underneath a rock formation, claiming the rock filtered the water. One of these days, we are going to hear about Bear Grylls being in the hospital with a pathogen infection. (He also has a nasty habit of eating raw trout he catches in the wild, which is a good way to get tapeworm.)

After the coarse filter removes the large impurities, I would then either boil or home-distill the water. If boiled, I would then run the water through a fine filter (even a coffee filter works for this). If distilled, the water will be safe for drinking without need of further filtering, assuming the collection vessel for the still is sanitary. If better tasting water is desired at that point, it can be aerated, salted, and chilled.

Heat

Heat is the most reliable and effective treatment for water. All living organisms (including all pathogens) die when water reaches temperatures of about 185 degrees Fahrenheit, but that temperature should be held for at least ten minutes. Also, effective sterilization temperatures and holding times will depend somewhat on your elevation and the barometric pressure. The higher you are and/or the lower the barometric pressure, the higher the temperature and/or holding time needs to be.

To be safe, just boil the water. Boiling kills everything for certain, regardless of the weather or your location, and the holding time only needs to be about a minute. Water boils at round 212 degrees Fahrenheit, but your mileage will vary. Fortunately, you don't need a thermometer and can visibly see when water boils. Longer boiling times are of no additional benefit, and just needlessly reduce your yield. The drawback to boiling is it removes all taste from the water, and of course there is also the challenge of sanitary storage after boiling. For that reason, water which is purified by boiling should generally be consumed soon thereafter, or combined with a filtration system before consumption.

To add taste back to boiled water, you can aerate it after it cools. Putting oxygen back into the water will improve its taste, but water cannot absorb oxygen at high temperatures.

Stir it vigorously with a sanitized spoon (for example, a metal one which was emerged in the boiling water), or seal it in a sterile container and shake the heck out of it. Another option is to use the boiled water to make Tang with and pretend you are an astronaut, getting a nice dose of Vitamin C in the process – but of course, you would need to have Tang stockpiled in order to do that, which defeats the purpose of off-grid living for many people.

One large reserve of safe drinking water most people have is in their hot water heater. In an emergency situation, this will come in handy, as we are talking about at least 40 gallons here. The water inside a residential water heater has been sufficiently heated to become sanitized, has been flowing through regularly, and is housed in a sanitary environment. To access it, you will need to first disconnect the power source to the unit, turning off the gas or disconnecting the electrical connections. Then, you can use the valve at the bottom of the tank to dispense the water as needed.

Be aware that the water inside a waterbed mattress is **not** safe to drink, and neither is the water inside your toilet tanks (unless first boiled and then preferably filtered as well).

Also, heat treatment will not sanitize water which has been contaminated by radioactivity or harmful chemicals.

Chemical Treatment

Municipal water supplies are made safe for human consumption by chemical treatment. It is the only practical large-scale solution. As an off-grid homesteader, this may be an option you want to look into, assuming you have a reliable source for obtaining the chemicals.

Plain old household bleach is the most common chemical used to treat water. It is also known as *liquid chlorine*, the same stuff that keeps swimming pools clean. Swimming pool water has been treated with much too much chlorine to be able to drink it, however. A little bleach goes a long way! The recommended treatment is only half a teaspoon for 5 gallons of clear water, or twice that if the water is cloudy. Make sure the water is warm when you add the bleach, as chlorine is ineffective at chilled temperatures. Test the treatment by smelling it. You should be able to detect a faint bleach/chlorine smell about an hour after adding it, which tells you the water is now safe. If the water started as cloudy, it should now be clear. If you can't smell any bleach at all, or if the water has not cleared, go ahead and give it another dose of bleach, same amount. If you still cannot detect the bleach smell after another hour goes by, discard the water, as it is too infected for the chlorine to sanitize it. Always start with the smaller dosage of bleach when doing this, and only double it if needed. Give the water some time and warm it up to over 65 degrees Fahrenheit before treating it, if the water is cool.

The most practical way to store chlorine bleach is in *Calcium Hypochlorite* granule form. This is a dry powder you can purchase at swimming pool supply stores. It is inexpensive and has a much longer shelf life than liquid bleach. It also has much better storage efficiency, taking up less space. You can make liquid bleach from it if you desire by mixing one ounce of it with one pint of water, but you can also sanitize your drinking water directly by adding just a tiny pinch of the stuff directly into a gallon of water, same procedure as sanitizing with liquid bleach. Make sure the water is warm.

Another effective water sanitizing chemical is iodine. This requires a slightly higher dosage than liquid bleach; use 8 drops per half-gallon for clear water, double that if the water is cloudy. The water needs to be warm as well, and the waiting time is approximately an hour. With iodine, the smell test is not available as it is with bleach, so you just have to trust it. If the water started as cloudy, it should be clear. Do not double the dosage, however, if the water fails to clear. Simply discard it. Some health risks are associated with long-term iodine exposure, and pregnant women / nursing mothers should avoid it entirely, as should those with thyroid conditions. For these reasons, iodine should be considered a short-term solution only.

Stores selling water purification tablets are simply selling you either chlorine or iodine in a tablet form. In my opinion, this is a fancy-packaged way of marketing inexpensive chemicals to the gullible. In addition, these tablets have a relatively short shelf life. They are obviously not a practical solution for off-grid homesteaders. Go with the *Calcium Hypochlorite* granules if you want to store up water purification chemicals.

Also, chemical treatment will not sanitize water which has been contaminated by radioactivity or harmful chemicals.

Filtering

Filtering drinking water is the most practical solution, as we have already touched upon somewhat, as long as the water is from a reasonably clean source such as a well. Modern water filters are very fine and will remove everything except certain viruses. Fortunately, viruses are not typically an issue with well water; bad well water is usually the result of a protozoan infection – and filters are effective in removing protozoa. In addition, filters will remove most harmful chemicals and even radioactive particles. Therefore, viruses can be removed by chemical treatment and then the chemicals used to treat the water can be filtered out of it.

In disaster survival situations, it is almost always human waste contaminating drinking water supplies which results in health epidemics. In these situations, you need to use multiple treatment methods in order to be safe, especially routines which involve boiling the water. If I were forced to consume water known to be significantly bad, I would first coarse-filter it through some kind of cloth (such as a cotton towel), then boil it, then treat it with a small dose of bleach, then run it through a fine filter.

Commercial water filters that are placed within residential plumbing lines require an outside energy force in order to work - usually either electricity or water pressure itself. A backup hand-pump for your well will ensure that you can always draw water from it, and also be able to create enough pressure to run it through your inline filter. Electric power can be supplied through the use of a portable solar generator, and/or rechargeable batteries which are kept charged by a portable solar generator while the sun is shining. So, there are two methods to make sure your inline water filters will always be usable.

Portable water filters, on the other hand, are either gravity-fed or function by a built-in hand pump, so do not rely upon an outside energy force. These are popular with disaster relief organizations and missionaries in third-world countries, especially the gravity-fed type (which are stainless steel table-top appliances weighing ten pounds or less without water). They resemble a coffee dispenser with a spout at the bottom. Reasonably-clear water is poured into the top. It is filtered inside the unit and good drinkable water comes out the spout at the bottom – simple, just like making coffee or tea. The two most widely-sold models of portable water filters are manufactured by companies *AquaRain* and *British Berkefeld*.

However you treat your water at home, remember to use the purified water when brushing your teeth or washing your face. (Most people use way too much toothpaste, just a small dollop is sufficient. Better yet, use baking soda to brush your teeth half of the time.)

Build Your Own Water Filter

One of the unattractive aspects of purifying water by filtering it is the dependency upon an industrialized society to continue to produce the replacement filters. Many off-gridders live in expectation of a total collapse of society, which may include a complete cessation of the manufacturing industries. Indeed, the very idea of living off the grid is to become self-sustainable, or at least self-sustainable enough to be able to trade with other local homesteaders for needed supplies.

To that end, you will probably be interested in learning about the properties of charcoal and silver. Many portable water filters incorporate both silver and charcoal elements. These are raw materials which can be stockpiled, or possibly even produced, by a community of homesteaders.

Silver is a natural sanitizing agent. It destroys pathogens which it comes into contact with. In the old west, they used to keep a silver dollar in the water barrels, not really understanding the whys of it, but knowing it was a reliable preventative health measure. Modern water filters usually contain fine silver particles which water must come into contact with as it passes through. As simple as that sounds, it works.

Charcoal does not destroy pathogens, but is a very effective filtering medium, being a fine porous granular material with a high surface area. When you hear the term "carbon filter" it is referring to a charcoal filter. It is important to understand that charcoal and coal are not the same thing. Coal is mined from the ground. Charcoal is what you get from burning wood at high temperatures in a concentrated form, especially in a low-oxygen environment (which fire itself creates). You actually produce charcoal every time you have a campfire. After a few hours, when you see those hot coals burning bright at the bottom of your wood fire, you can douse the fire out with water and will have a small supply of usable charcoal.

You can create a water filter in the wild using nothing more than sand, small rocks, and the charcoal from your campfire. You should have some kind of a funnel-shaped vessel to create it in, such as a large plastic funnel or an upside down empty half-gallon plastic bottle (especially an empty bleach bottle, after it has been rinsed out well with hot water). Boil the rocks first, or heat them in a fire until they glow. When they cool, put a layer of them at the bottom of your funnel to hold the charcoal and sand. Then add a layer of charcoal and a layer of sand, and repeat the charcoal/sand layers until you fill the funnel. That's it. You can now filter reasonably clean-looking water through your device and drink it. If you have some silver dust, even better - sprinkle some of it between the bottom layer of charcoal and sand. As an alternative, you could place some pure silver coins in that layer instead (in the USA, pure silver coins have dates of 1964 or before). If you don't include the silver in your filter, I would boil or chemically treat the water before running it through the filter.

You can, of course, simply purchase activated charcoal granules at most hardware stores and use those instead. Additionally, you can stuff clean cotton balls in the neck of your funnel for one final level of filtering.

For a more industrialized solution, you can create your own water filter system using replacement water filter cartridges. All you need is two food-grade storage containers of the same size, such as those white 5-gallon plastic buckets that many home-brewers use for primary fermentation vessels. You will also need a rubber O-ring and a nut that fits on the filter cartridge unit. Drill a hole in the bottom of one of the buckets the size of the threaded end of the water filter cartridge. Put the cartridge inside that bucket, and stick the threaded end through the hole, placing the O-ring between the cartridge and the bottom of the bucket to seal the hole. Tighten the nut on the outside of the bottom of the bucket to secure it. You're finished. Sit the bucket with the filter over the other bucket, and fill the top bucket with water. The drinkable, filtered water will fill the bottom container.

Harvesting H2o

Home Distillation

Distilled water is water that is turned into vapor form, and then collected as it turns back into liquid through the process of condensation. To turn the water to vapor, it is boiled, but the resulting steam is captured and trapped in a vessel which forces it to condensate, and the condensation is then harvested. The vaporization process removes all impurities, and in fact all chemical elements from the water, resulting in pure H_2O.

Making distilled water on your stove is fairly simple to accomplish, but it typically consumes a lot of energy. It's been said by the U.S. government that for every gallon of distilled water produced, a gallon of fuel is consumed. That was referring to making it on the road in wartime, however. These days, the energy supply can be a basic electric stovetop powered by solar panels, an infinitely renewable source.

Because distilled water is void of minerals, there is some health concern over using it as a primary, long-term source of drinking water. You can always replenish some of those minerals by adding a tiny bit of salt to each glass you drink.

There are several reasons why a homesteader may be interested in distilling water. The most obvious is that this method will create potable water from even the most contaminated sources, and will even convert saltwater into drinking water! Also, some people need distilled water for various mechanical uses. Here are several ways you can make your own distilled water.

A very simple method is to simply harvest steam from a tea kettle. There are many creative ways in which you might do this. One way that I have witnessed uses a thick food-grade plastic tube inserted into the neck of the kettle and the other end stuck through a hole cut near the top of a disposable plastic cup (the kind used for picnics). Seal the top of the cup with plastic wrap and also stuff some plastic wrap in the edges of the hole that the tube comes through. At the tea kettle end, you will need to remove the plastic cap from the kettle spout to fit the tube into it. Seal this end with wadded up paper towels stuffed around the tube. When the water starts to boil, the steam will come through the tube into the cup. After a couple minutes you will have about a third of the cup filled with distilled water; you can then turn off the heat and remove the plastic wrap from the cup. The volume will increase over the next ten minutes as the condensation from the sides of the cup runs down into it.

A slightly more practical method involves a pot, a glass bowl which barely fits inside the pot, some ice, and a lid to a bigger pot. Fill the pot about halfway with water and float the glass bowl in the water. Heat the water. When it gets hot, put the lid to the other pot upside-down on top of the pot and pile ice on top of the lid. Let the water in the pot boil for a while. Turn the heat off and remove the lid (using mitts of course). Inside the pot will be a glass bowl full of distilled water. Be careful to allow the glass bowl to cool slowly, or it will break.

Finally, you can use a pressure cooker to home-distill water. This is the most practical method if you need a decent yield. You will need a good length of copper tubing for this, at least ten feet. You will also need a chair, a large plastic bucket, and a clean food-grade container for collecting the distilled water. The plastic bucket will be for cooling, so you will need to form a coil out of the middle of the copper tubing inside the bucket. This is much easier to do if you have an object in the shape of a cylinder to wrap the copper tube around, such as one of those large tins that Christmas treats are packaged in. The plastic bucket goes on the chair, which is placed next to the stove, with the copper coil inside. One end of the copper tubing then goes into the collection vessel, which sits on the floor. The other end goes into the exhaust hole in the lid of your pressure cooker, about 2/3 filled with water on your stovetop, and should fit snugly into the opening (if it doesn't, you can stuff around it with wadded up paper towels).

Fill the plastic bucket with cold water. Turn the pressure cooker on. As the water heats, it will turn into steam and be forced through the copper tubing exhaust pipe. When it goes through the coil in the cold water bucket, it will condensate and be turned back into water. Distilled water will exit into your collection vessel on the floor. Once the distilled water begins to output, the heat can be reduced on the stove and it will improve the yield (but also take longer to produce). Be very, very careful not to touch the hot section of the copper tubing once the steam starts going through it with your bare hands, or you may suffer severe burns! Same goes for the pressure cooker, naturally. Use those potholders! Let everything cool naturally when you are done. Seal the collection vessel quickly, or transfer the distilled water to sanitized storage containers and seal them.

If you are distilling water from a contaminated source (or distilling saltwater) it should be coarse-filtered first through something like a clean cotton cloth or bed sheet. After distilling, clean the tea kettle, cooking pot, or pressure cooker which held the pre-distilled water diligently using an anti-bacterial soap. Do the same for your hands afterward. Launder the cloth used for filtering immediately. The copper tubing does not need to be cleaned, because it only came into contact with the pure steam and clean distilled water.

Land-Based Marine Water Makers

Most yachts and sailboats over 20 feet long have a water maker on board, known as a *desalination system,* which converts seawater into safe drinking water. They have an input which sucks in water from below the boat, strains it into fresh drinking water, delivers it to a tank (usually connected to an onboard faucet), dumps the leftover bad stuff back into the sea, and then takes in more saltwater to repeat the process on a continuous basis. This process has a yield ratio of about 10/90, resulting in a volume of 10% of the saltwater taken in output as freshwater, and the rest dumped back out.

Theoretically, as environmentalists may point out, the world's oceans would eventually become more concentrated from this process, possibly killing off sea life and eventually destroying the world, to say nothing of the ever-decreasing water maker output yield from the desalination process. That theory may be seriously flawed, however, and would take millions of years to test with a lot more water makers running than could ever practically be produced. Besides, man also dumps a considerable amount of fresh water (albeit most in the form of waste) back into the oceans as well.

The way these devices work is through *reverse osmosis*. This is a highly-pressurized filtration process, using a very fine filtering membrane which is capable of removing the smallest micro-particles including salt, most minerals, and all pathogens including viruses. The bad water enters one side of a two-compartment vessel separated by the membrane, to which high pressure is then applied, forcing pure fresh water to filter through the membrane, leaving salt and everything else behind in the first compartment. The first compartment is then flushed and replenished with a new supply of bad water to filter.

These devices have been used in marine applications since they were invented in the middle of the twentieth century. Starting in the 1970's, they were also marketed as a freshwater filtration system to create softer, better-tasting drinking water in homes and workplace environments. A freshwater reverse osmosis system is differently calibrated and cannot effectively be used for desalination, though. (The reverse, however, is not true; a desalination system can certainly be used to filter fresh water.) This is because freshwater reverse osmosis systems require less pressure and typically use a coarser membrane to filter through, in an effort to improve yield efficiency. To desalinate saltwater, very high pressure and a fine membrane is required, but of course that results in a much less efficient yield.

Land-based desalination systems are now readily available due to demand from both residential and commercial customers, not to mention off-grid homesteaders. Many of these systems are expensive and require contractor installation, such as the models sold by Ech2o Tec and Village Marine. They are large and designed to be stationary applications with an unlimited saltwater supply being pumped in. Seaside resorts, military stations, and owners of fancy waterfront homes will pay between $5,000 and $25,000 to have one installed. This may be a workable solution for certain financially-blessed off-gridders who are coastally situated or have salt marshes in their vicinity.

For most of us, however, a portable marine water maker will make much more sense. In fact, this is a reasonable emergency kit item to have for anyone who lives near a large body of saltwater. I have seen them for sale on Amazon and eBay starting at about $600. Manufacturer brand names include Katadyn, Ampac, and Spectra. The more compact models are used in lifeboats and can operate from volumes as small as a bucket of water. In a prolonged disaster situation, one person on your street who happens to have one of these could save the entire block.

If you are going to store one of these devices, it would be prudent to also have appropriate reservoir containers on hand. Remember, the volume of output is very small when desalinating saltwater. A child's inflatable swimming pool would be a good thing to have filled for the input side, with a 5-gallon food-grade plastic bucket for the output. The labor of transporting enough saltwater to fill an inflatable pool is something to consider. It's a good idea to engineer all this based on your proximity to the saltwater supply, in advance.

The other consideration is power. The smaller units, designed for life rafts, are hand-pumped. Some also include a rechargeable battery system which can be used as an alternative to the hand pump, which is a great convenience, being as you can only produce about a pint of water from an hour of hand-pumping. That is just about enough water to quench the thirst worked up from an hour of pumping!

The really nice thing about a reverse osmosis system is you don't need to concern yourself over replacement filters. The membrane inside the unit should last a lifetime. Yes, you may choose to run desalinated water through an additional freshwater filter to improve its taste, but that is just a luxury. The output water from any marine water maker is safe to drink directly.

Drill Your Own Well

There is perhaps no more satisfying feeling than pumping clear water from a new backyard well you drilled yourself. When that bright, beautiful liquid spills over your land for the first time, you may become exhilarated realizing that the unlimited supply you just tapped into is forever free. Most home-dug backyard wells can produce 2-3 gallons per minute on demand, and many have a flow rate of several times that. Accessing groundwater yourself is not terribly difficult. In underdeveloped nations, wells are still drilled by hand without the aid of modern machinery.

There is a difference between *well water* and *groundwater*. Well water is what you get from a professionally-drilled well. These are deep; typically 200–500 feet. Such deep-source water is usually safe to drink right from the well. Unfortunately, you cannot drill this type of well yourself and will need to hire the pros to come out with a commercial drilling rig. Be prepared to spend at least $4,000 for a proper well in most areas.

Groundwater, however, is most likely accessible a mere 10-30 feet under your homestead. You just need to go down there and get it. A groundwater well is also referred to as a *shallow well*. The water they produce is not generally considered potable. For that reason, most people who dig shallow wells do so for irrigation and cleaning purposes. That being said, knowing what you already know, this is a renewable source of reasonably clear water which can then be purified by one of the methods discussed in the previous chapters.

In third-world countries, water from shallow wells is commonly consumed straight from the ground, as it has been for thousands of years in all different cultures. It wasn't until deep-well drilling techniques became possible from the industrial revolution in the 20th century that shallow groundwater was considered unsafe. Don't ask me why. In ancient times, very large wells were dug, big enough to fit a team of diggers down the hole. If you go to Israel, you can see a Biblical relic at the city of Beersheba, which is supposed to be the well that Abraham dug in the book of Genesis. It is 12-feet wide and 50 feet deep, and was dug through a layer of limestone. Your backyard project will be much easier.

You should, of course, send a water sample from any well in for testing before consuming it. There is a pretty good chance the test from your own shallow well will come back as safe to drink, but do get it tested. Even if it does test as safe, I still advise purifying the water before drinking it. A home-dug well can become contaminated much easier than a deep well, so habitually purifying the water and having it retested often is highly advised.

Many people mistakenly think of groundwater as an underwater river or lake. That is only true in the case of springs. For the most part, groundwater is just a marshy earth layer which is located between other layers of earth. When you get down to the wet stuff, you will find coarser soil the deeper you go in that layer, until you are at a level of coarse sand. That is where the water can most easily be extracted, so that is the target for our shallow well. To get there, we need to first find the *water table*, go through marshy mud, and then a fine layer of sand (sometimes referred to as *water-bearing sand*). Beyond the fine sand, we get to the coarse sand where we end our drilling. If we go too far beyond that, we may hit another level of hard ground.

The hard ground that you must go through before arriving at the wet layer varies in texture regionally. In Michigan, you may have nice, easy, soft, muddy ground that you can slice through like a cake. In Missouri, you will probably find hard clay that you must slowly grind your way through. Down along the gulf coast, the ground is mostly sand, which sounds easy, but can present its own challenges (like frequent cave-ins). You should get an idea of the ground type in your area before you decide which home-drilling technique to try first. The best way to get this information is from other homesteaders in the area who have drilled their own shallow wells. You can also ask local professional drilling companies or specialty hardware stores who sell drilling equipment.

The other piece of information you need before you start is the local water table level. This is the layer in the ground where you first hit wet soil. The top area of this level will not provide good water, as it will be very muddy and marshy – but it will still have a primarily liquid consistency. The water table location is not an exact known place and can only really be determined by drilling, but it's good to know whether your neighbors found water at 9 feet or 22 feet to give you an idea of what to expect. One website which may help is the United States Geological Survey site at USGS.gov. Search for the term "water table" followed by your county. You also may be able to get this information from local drilling businesses or rural family-owned hardware stores.

Drilling your own shallow well can be done quite inexpensively, although there is a good deal of manual labor involved in the process. There are several popular techniques you can employ, but they all involve boring a deep, small-diameter hole in the ground by the use of hand tools. The possible hazards include getting your drill pipe stuck, hitting rocks that are too big to be broken up, and your hole caving in. The only one of these problems which is unsolvable is the case of hitting hard rock. Usually rocks can be busted up and removed from the bore hole. One effective method for breaking rocks is dropping a heavy metal object into the hole tied to a rope, over and over. If you hit bedrock, however, you are done and will need to start over in a new location. (Bedrock is the hardest layer of earth and is not negotiable. Fortunately, the odds are slim that you will encounter it before you strike water.)

Most of the time when people think they hit hard rock they really just hit hard clay. Hard clay can be bored through by hand, even with plastic PVC pipe. You just have to keep working it. Don't give up every time the going gets slow! I can almost guarantee there will be some slow patches, and the slowest one should be just before you hit the water table.

Whichever method you use for boring the hole, the goal is the same: To insert a *well screen* at the bottom of the hole in the coarse sand level, which will be attached to your well-casing pipe. A well screen is simply a coarse filter, usually made from either a wire mesh or simply thin slots cut in the bottom of the sealed pipe. This screen keeps large particles in the ground out of your drawn water. The well screen is typically at least several feet in length, and the top of it must be submerged far enough below the water table to be safe from ever coming above it – because if it does, the well screen will suck air and stop the pump from working. You may also wish to surround your well screen with a packing of small gravel, which will improve your well's performance and provide an additional layer of filtering.

Another term you should be familiar with is the *well point*, which is simply a well screen with a point on the end, useful for penetrating at least some degree of ground (or gravel) when planting it.

It is more important to understand the concept behind well drilling than to follow a step-by-step set of instructions. That way, you can call an audible if need be and may be able to save your partially-drilled well with a bit of ingenuity when you run into problems. Many backyard well drillers started off using one method and ended up switching to a different one in order to finish the job.

Choosing a good spot for the well is important. It must be located at least 100 feet away from all sewage/septic lines (including garbage dumps or trash storage areas) and at least 50 feet away from any animal pens. It should be on an upward slope from your septic tank, if possible. Hopefully your land is not too hilly, as groundwater wells work best in flatter areas. Don't be afraid of drilling under a tree, especially a large one. Large trees indicate that a decent water source is close by, and roots are easy to bore through. Having your water pump located in the shade can also be a plus. Just be cognizant of the need to occasionally have long pipes over your head while working, and remove any tree branches beforehand which figure to become obstacles during the process.

The problem of cave-ins can be avoided by keeping the boring pipe in the ground until a smaller diameter well casing pipe is in place;

or, by using drilling fluid in the hole. Drilling fluid is usually made with *Bentonite*, which can be purchased via the brand names *Aquagel* or *Quick-gel*. Bentonite actually forms hard clay when mixed sufficiently with water, but for making drilling fluid less of it is used (just enough to thicken water). This thickened water is put down into the boring hole where it keeps the hole from caving in on itself. When the well is complete, the drilling fluid is flushed out.

The ground type and estimated water table level will affect the diameter of the hole you need to bore, which in turn will affect the drilling method you should choose. This is because a regular hand pump which works on suction, such as a pitcher pump, can only draw water from a maximum depth of 25 feet. This is an atmospheric pressure issue and cannot be changed. Therefore, if the water table is deeper than 25 feet, you will need to use a submersible pump (or another solution such as a jet stream pump) and those require a greater diameter well casing to fit down inside of. Please note that the depth of your well doesn't matter so much as the water table level, since your well casing pipe will naturally fill to whatever level the water table is at. If you figure on needing to use a submersible pump, plan on having a well casing pipe of at least 4 inches in diameter. Most home-drilled wells find water closer than 25 feet and have a well casing pipe no bigger than 2 inches in diameter, hooked to a regular hand pump.

After the well is drilled to the desired depth, it's time to flush the muddy water and drilling fluid out of the hole. This can be done with a simple suction-siphon technique, by thrusting a long pipe up and down continually at the bottom of the hole until water starts flushing out the top of the pipe over your head. Usually the pipe has an angled end-cap pointed away from the person doing the thrusting, so as not to soak them. If this doesn't work the first time, fill the flushing pipe with water after it is submerged and that will start the siphon process for you.

Once the flushing is producing clear water, the well casing pipe with the attached well screen can be planted. The hole then needs to be filled and sealed in order to prevent contamination from above. Fill the hole around the well casing pipe with sand until you are reasonably sure you are above the water table. Then fill the rest of it with either cement or Benzonite (a thicker solution than the drilling fluid which will harden into clay). Fill the well casing pipe with water to in order to prime the pump, attach your hand pump, and pump until you have clear well water coming out. Voila, you have a well. If your pump does not include a one way valve, known as a *check valve*, insert one at the top of your pipe, but first install a T-section which will allow you to prime the pump below the check valve and then seal the T section off. This is all to prevent surface water from contaminating the well.

Auger Drilling

The simplest method of digging a well is simply digging it out using an extendable auger, the size used for post-holes (usually a 6" auger). This will only get you so far, however, and they become increasingly difficult to use the deeper you get. After about ten feet you will be lucky if you are strong enough to still turn it. I have seen videos of complete wells bored out using only an auger, but they were very shallow with water tables located no more than 10-12 feet. Normally, the well must be finished by using another drilling method. For all practical purposes, I would figure on using a post auger to dig a starter hole of no more than 7-8 feet and then continue from there with a different method.

If you are able to hit water at about 10 feet or so with the auger, that is shallow enough to probably be able to avoid cave-ins and you might be able to just finish the well with the auger. You need to get down below the water table by at least a few feet though, and the digging will now be slower because you will have at least some mudslide caving at the bottom of the hole. I would suggest putting the auger away at this point and inserting about 15 feet of 6-inch PVC pipe. This can be also function as your well pipe casing, if you wish. Once the PVC pipe hits bottom, begin flushing the mud out by thrusting a long thin pipe as described above. As you flush, you will be able to keep pushing the PVC pipe lower. When it gets to the ground, you will know you are five feet below the water table and can use that as a bucket-style well, or you can add another 5-foot section to the PVC pipe and go even deeper.

I would probably add another five-foot section at that point and try for another couple of feet of depth at least. As a much better alternative to a bucket-style well, a smaller-diameter PVC pipe with a well point fitted to the end can be inserted down the pipe all the way to the bottom, and then pea gravel filled in between the outer and inner pipes for a few feet. I would then probably remove the outer pipe casing and add a bit more gravel, then a large layer of sand, and then top up with cement. Finish the well by priming the pipe and attaching a hand pump. This should be a very productive well, going 7-8 feet below the water table and having a surrounding gravel pack at the well screen – especially if you use a large diameter well casing pipe such as 2-3 inches.

Driving a Well Point

A very popular method of backyard well drilling is not drilling at all, but swinging a sledge hammer to drive a well point to water. This method is a bit dicey, but probably worth a shot if you live in a flat area with reasonably soft ground and expect to find water at 20 feet or less. The type of well point used in this method is known as a *sand point*; a strong, metal piece containing a wire mesh well screen. It is fitted unto a narrow metal pipe, usually no bigger than 2 inches in diameter, which means you must use a suction-pump and therefore need to have a water table closer than 25 feet. A driven sand point will break up most small rocks it encounters without damaging the piece, but if you hit hard red clay your drilling attempt is probably done (and in all probability, you must sacrifice the sand point and the pipe in the ground).

If you expect to go down less than 20 feet, use 1.25" pipe; use 2" diameter pipe if you expect to go further. Metal piping is used in this method, usually in 5 foot lengths. Do not hit the pipe with the hammer! A small piece of equipment known as a *drive cap* is fitted over the end and that is what you strike. When the pipe gets down to the ground, remove the drive cap, screw on another 5' length of pipe, put the dive cap on that end, and continue swinging. You will need something to stand on when starting off on a new length of pipe, such as the tailgate of a pickup truck.

You won't know when you hit water except by trial and error, so when you think you are getting down to the water table try filling the pipe with water. If you cannot fill it up to where the water level remains full at the top of the pipe, you are not there yet. Repeat every few feet until the pipe can be filled and retains water. When it can, attach a pump to it temporarily and make sure you actually have water and not debris caught in the pipe somewhere. If the holding water pumps out and then you have muddy water, great. If not, put a long thin rod (or smaller diameter piping) down the pipe to try and free whatever is caught in it. As an alternative way to see if you have hit water, you could just insert a long piece of wire to the bottom of the pipe and then pull it up to see if the end is wet.

Once you have water pumping, go several feet deeper if you can, and you are done. Attach the pump and pump it until the water runs clear. You have a well. As you can see, the

59

main attraction of this method is the simplicity of it, just drive down a pipe and hook up a pump. However, oftentimes this method goes awry because of large rocks or hard clay.

Washing in a Well

The other techniques for home well-drilling are all water-oriented and are collectively known as *washing*. This is a very effective method and can get past hard clay, and even larger rocks sometimes with a little determination. The bore hole is scraped by hand-twisting or stabbing a jagged-edge end of a pipe or piece of tubing, while water is used to continuously bring the *cuttings* to the surface of the hole where they wash aside.

There are two basic methods for washing the bore hole. You either shoot the water down the inside of the drilling pipe, bringing the cuttings up from the outside (that is, between the drill pipe and the outer diameter of the hole), or you pour water down the hole and flush everything out through the top of the drill pipe, as already has been described. Either way, the bore hole is larger than the diameter of the drill pipe due to the constant moving and twisting of it. Sections of pipe are added as needed while the drill pipe goes lower into the ground.

PVC Pipe Drilling

Water pressure can be an issue with this method. Be prepared to use a heck of a lot of water to drill your well this way, unless you have access to a mud pump, in which case you can recirculate the water. For the first 10-15 feet, you don't need much water pressure, but as you go deeper, it will take more than one garden hose to flush out the cuttings. The solution is to use two garden hoses, a mud pump recirculation system, or use an air hose in conjunction with one garden hose (which will increase the pressure enough to use the water from one hose).

One end of the first piece of PVC pipe will be your drill bit. Cut triangular teeth into the end of it, or screw in a metal end-piece with jagged teeth cut into it. If screwing in a metal end-piece for the drill bit, you will need to secure it with a screw through the side of the pipe to keep it from unscrewing as you drill.

61

Keep in mind plenty of wells have been drilled this way using only plastic teeth cut into the PVC pipe itself. Whichever way you make the drilling end sharp, make the teeth large with lots of room between them, and keep the inside of the end of the pipe clear and open! Eventually, you need to run your smaller well casing pipe (with a well point fixed on the end of it) through the end of your drill pipe.

On the other end of the drilling pipe a T-section cap fits on, which is securely fitted with two garden hoses coming in each end of it, or one garden hose and one air hose. Turn the water on, put the drill pipe into the starter hole, and start twisting. Keep twisting. That is what you will be doing for hours on end, twisting and wiggling that pipe. This will bore a hole in the ground which is a little bigger in diameter than the drill pipe. You will need to fasten a removable handle of some type to the drill pipe, such as a thin, strong piece of wood held on by hose clamps. The pipe will go down to the ground, and then you will need to turn off the water, remove the T-head (with the hoses) and the handle attachment, then couple in a new section of PVC pipe. Use inside couplers and use both PVC primer and glue when attaching. Give it a few minutes to dry, then attach the T-head and the handle assembly to the new section of pipe, turn the water back on, and repeat.

Go slow once you get past 12 feet or so. Trying to go too fast can get your pipe stuck. When you hit hard ground and think you stopped making progress, just keep at it, and keep going slow. If you become absolutely sure you hit rock, drop a heavy metal object tied to a rope down the pipe over and over, trying to break it up. If that fails, put a little Bentonite solution down the hole and remove the entire drilling pipe and try smashing the rock up without the pipe in the hole. Re-sharpen the teeth of the drill pipe, or add a metal tip to it, and attempt to continue. Most likely, you will get through it.

This process can be greatly improved by using a mud pump instead of two garden hoses. In this case, you just have a single attachment at the top of the open drill pipe section, connected to the mud pump output hose. Dig a pit in the ground next to the well hole and connect it to the well hole with a small trench.

Fill the pit with a Bentonite solution and place a barbeque grill over the bottom of the pit, allowing for a few inches of the pit below the grill. Place the intake of the mud pump in the pit over the grill. You can now pump your drilling fluid down the drill pipe and it will recirculate and leave the cuttings in the mud pit under the barbeque grill. You will need to add extra water/drilling fluid at first and occasionally stop to shovel out the cuttings under the grill.

At some point, you will hit the water-bearing sand you are looking for. It will just start pouring out the sides of the top of the hole. At first it will be fine. You want to go a few feet deeper to find the coarser sand. When you do, you can stop twisting the drill pipe and you should be able to watch it sink further without any pressure on it at all. That is when you have arrived.

Piece together the entire well casing pipe ahead of time. Keep track of how many sections of drill pipe you sank, so you know your depth, and finish off the well casing pipe to be the same length. When it is all glued together with the well point sealed on the end, sink it all down inside the drill tube to the bottom. Lifting a long section of PVC pipe may be (at least) a two-man job, but fortunately it will bend quite a bit, and you may want to lay it over a high object such as the cab of your truck. When the well casing pipe is down, you can pour pea gravel down the inside of the drill pipe tube and slowly begin to pull it out, if you like, until you have a layer of several feet of gravel poured in. Then remove the drill pipe completely, add sand, and top off with cement. Prime the well casing pipe and hook up your pump. Nice well.

If the water table is expected to be within 25 feet, use 2" pipe for drilling and 1.25" pipe for the well casing. Otherwise, remember you will need a 4" pipe for well casing which means drilling with at least 5" diameter PVC pipe. Using larger diameter pipe and going deeper means going slower, and the process will be more arduous.

Flush Drilling

This is the opposite method for washing in a well, where you flush out the cuttings through the inside of the drill pipe – which is usually a metal pipe with a removable elbow-cap on the top end, positioned so the flushing spays away from the driller. You extend it by adding more sections as you go, always moving the bent end-cap to the top of the new section. The drill tip usually resembles a spear, except that it is fashioned above the hollow drill pipe so the flushings can get into the pipe. Water pressure and suction force the flushings to siphon out the top as the driller continually thrusts the drill pipe into the muddy hole.

To start, water must be added to the starter hole in order to create mud, and frequently be replenished. So, the ground is essentially turned to mud, ground up by the spear, and flushed out through the tube. After going down ten feet or so, a Bentonite solution should be used instead of water, as this method of drilling has a high danger of cave-ins due to there being no supporting pipe in the drill hole.

When mixing Bentonite, be swirling the water before adding the powder. Mix it in a bucket first before pouring it down the bore hole.

When you get past 18 feet or so, the driller will probably need help. If necessary, multiple people can then do the thrusting of the drill pipe in unison. It also may help to have somebody at a higher level pull the drill pipe up using a rope, so that the thrusters only need to thrust downward. For that purpose, a makeshift derrick is sometimes constructed above the drill hole with a pulley. The people pulling the drill pipe upward can then work from the ground.

When the sandy, clearer water flushes out the drill pipe, you have reached your destination. At that point, you can sink a well point connected to a long pipe and seal up the well. Many wells in third-world countries are dug by missionaries in this fashion.

Harvesting H2o

Collecting Rain

Collecting rainfall to meet ones water consumption needs is not a new idea. People have been doing it for thousands of years. In lifeboat emergency kits, you will sometimes find large folded-up plastic tarps which are intended to be unfolded and used as rain collection devices during storms (this was especially true in the days before portable marine water makers). Sailors who became shipwrecked on islands have used the large leaves from banana trees and other tropical plants to capture rainwater and direct it into collection vessels.

In many regions, a bountiful harvest of water can be collected during rainstorms and then stored for later usage. You just have to be ready for it when it happens. Using rainwater as a supplemental supply can significantly increase the life of your other water-producing resources. For example, your shallow well may last 25 years instead of 15. No wonder collecting rainwater is rapidly gaining interest with today's off-grid homesteaders.

Rainwater is collected from wide surface areas and then funneled into storage containers. The simplest method is to have the rain gutters from the roof of your home empty into collection barrels. If you have multiple structures on your property (including sheds and carports), put roofs with rain gutters over all of them and direct the gutters into barrels. You can also build additional structures specifically designed for capturing rainfall, which are really nothing more than overhead shelters. Water collected in this method will be more contaminated than water from other sources due to coming in contact with the roof and rain gutters. That makes it a good candidate for distillation if you plan on treating it to become potable.

Otherwise, most rain barrels are used for watering gardens and livestock.

The primary challenge in collecting rain is that you need square footage in order to do it. Rain comes down in measurable inches, but you can only capture those inches with however wide of a collection area you have. If you need to collect more, you must use a wider collection space. Building a deeper collection vessel does nothing to increase your yield.

Fortunately, the roof of any decent-sized home will actually yield quite a bit of water. To give you an idea, the runoff created by an inch of rain on a 1,000 square foot roof will typically yield more than 600 gallons of water. That's a lot. What you want to do is maximize your collection efficiency. Most homes are guttered only at the low points of the roof, allowing a lot of runoff to escape over the higher edges. This can be fixed by guttering the entire roof, but that may create an aesthetic issue with some folks. As an alternative, you could put up short upward metal railings along the edges of the non-guttered roof sides, which will guide most of the runoff down to the gutters. Or, you can simply gutter more structures on your property, and maybe put up a new carport to harvest rain from.

That leaves us with the fun part: rain barrel design. Rain barrels are just plain cool. Making them is a rather easy project which allows for a great degree of individual tailoring. The best ones I have seen involve multiple vessels which overflow into one another, the last barrel in line being equipped with an overflow spout. I would set up a multi-barrel system like this under each structure you intend to capture rain from. In the case of a small shed, one large barrel may do, as long as you are additionally capturing the runoff from your house with a multi-barrel setup.

The barrel itself can be plastic, metal, wood, or PVC. I am partial to food-grade containers, whichever way you go (if wooden, you can use old wine or whiskey casks), especially if you will be using the water in a vegetable garden. The holding capacity of the vessel is a concern. Go with at least 50-gallon size containers. I have seen some really cool

72

setups made from 110-gallon metal food-grade drums. Because of the impressive volume of rain runoff, you will occasionally have storms where your overflow valve is reached no matter how large your system is – so think big.

Filter the incoming runoff water with a screen of some sort. Regular window screen works great, because it is fine enough to keep mosquitos out of the barrels. All other leaves and particles will also be filtered out, and will accumulate on top of the screen and eventually clog your filter – so you must clear it between storms, and maybe change the screen occasionally. On the system with the 110-gallon metal drums I mentioned, a shower drain plate was installed as a filter, which was neat-looking, but not fine enough to keep insects out. I saw one rain barrel that was made out of a plastic garbage can; a window screen covered the entire top of the can, and a hole was cut in the lid of the trash can to place the end of the rain gutter in.

You want a large enough intake opening to keep from losing water by overflow, but you also want the barrel to be as sealed as possible in order to keep the loss from evaporation at a minimum. A screened hand-sized opening on the top of the barrel is probably optimal for the intake, especially if the barrel has a lip around the top to capture overflow when the water is gushing at a high rate. You can, of course, install such a lip if one does not exist by using a bit of ingenuity (perhaps via clay or a metal ring or a combination).

You need to cut some holes and install some pipes or tubes. PVC pipe is great, but hose or rubber tubing also works. Whatever method you use, it must be waterproof and sealed. If only using one barrel, all you need is an overflow output at the top and a flow valve at the bottom (other than the screened intake opening on the top). Otherwise, install an overflow line near the top of the first barrel into the second, and repeat until the last barrel in line, where the overflow output simply spills unto the ground. Put flow valves at the bottom of each barrel. During a heavy rainstorm, you will fill all the barrels in your line and overflow will spill from the last vessel. A lighter rain may fill only the first barrel or two. Use the water sequentially, draining it from the flow valve of the last barrel in line which still contains water.

An alternative method would be to put the overflow lines at the bottom of each barrel (except the last). This setup works better if the barrels are on sloping ground, with the last one in line being at the lowest point. All the barrels will always have about the same amount of water in them. Because the system is somewhat gravity-fed, you only need to install a flow valve on the last barrel. In this arrangement, you need overflow valves installed at the tops of each barrel.

Install pipe fittings on your flow valves that you can hook a hose up to. What a great way to water your garden.

Want to collect even more rain water? Get a couple of children's inflatable swimming pools. A good rainstorm will put maybe 50 gallons of water into each of these, and it will be much less contaminated than the roof runoff water.

If you don't wish to build additional structures just to collect rainwater, but do want the ability of collecting more, you can fashion temporary structures using plastic tarps. Even a small 12 by 12 foot tarp may collect enough water in a rainstorm to overflow a 110-gallon barrel. The tarp should be well supported on the sides and have its low spot in the center, where a hole in it has been cut, and the collection vessel placed underneath. Try to position the tarp holders securely where the wind from the storm will not be able to disrupt them.

In an emergency situation, clean bed sheets can be hung from clothes lines and then rung out into a stopped up kitchen sink after the storm passes. This will probably not yield more than a couple of gallons, but the water should be drinkable as-is.

Other Sources of Water in the Wild

This section mainly applies to survival situations, but is good information to keep on hand. If you are an off-grid homesteader, you can probably drill a well or two and collect rainwater from your roof, and never have to worry about your water supply needs beyond that. The one possible exception to this lies in the harvesting of spring water, so we will start there. I have read the accounts of some homesteaders who depend on springs entirely for their supply of drinking water. While I don't think this is really all that wise, and would recommend drilling and rainwater collection instead, it does prove that it can be done.

If you have a spring creek running through your land (or nearby in the wild) that is a wonderful thing. The flow can dry up during hot summer months, however. When that happens, you may be able to pick it up again by digging down several feet at the lowest point of the dry creek bed. Otherwise, you will need to trace the spring to the source, up in the nearby hills most likely. Just follow the creek bed up. At some point you will probably find the bed of the creek getting muddy, and beyond that a trickle still running above ground. Keep going. At that point, you may as well to go all the way to the source, known as the head of the spring, where it first comes out of the ground. Water collected from the head of a spring is usually safe to drink without treatment, but get it tested first by bringing a sample to your county's local water service.

If you live in a hilly or mountainous area, you can probably find springheads year-round by tracing running creeks up into the highland. To find a running creek, start in the very lowlands. Water naturally seeks the lowest point by gravity. So, go down into the lowest valley, find a running stream or creek, and follow it up into the hills and mountains until you come to the source. One bit of warning: Don't do this immediately after a rain, because there will be many temporary springheads which will vanish in a day or two.

It should also be noted that the presence of springheads indicate a low water table, so very shallow wells can be dug nearby using only a post-hole auger.

As you are walking through the woods, you will likely discover other sources of water. You probably already know that stagnant water is highly contaminated, but in reality all surface water is contaminated to some degree. The safest water you will find in the wild, other than directly capturing rain in a sanitized vessel, is at the head of a spring. The next safest source would be very fast-moving water over rocks, such as from creeks and streams at higher elevations. I wouldn't drink that without treating it first, however.

Even stagnant water from the woods can, of course, be distilled or filtered through a reverse osmosis system (such as a marine

79

water maker) to create drinking water. Therefore, ponds and wildlife watering holes can become a usable source of wild water. Just be aware that such water is completely undrinkable and will probably make you very sick if consumed without properly treating it first.

After a rainstorm, water can be found holding in very small ponds at the tops of boulders, or in the depressions in rocky outcrops. Rainwater trapped in rock depressions is a cleaner source than a lake or a natural pond in the ground, but it still needs to be treated because it will contain insects and bird waste. If you have areas of rock outcrops nearby, they can be a good source of water after it rains.

Snow and ice can be a source of water, but the yield is quite low. It must be collected and hauled back to your home and placed in a melting vessel, such as a stopped up sink or a bucket next to your fireplace. Boil it before consuming it. You have heard the expression *don't eat the yellow snow*, right? You actually shouldn't eat *any* snow. It is unsafe and is not a source of hydration; in fact, consuming snow can cause dehydration. Melt it and boil it first.

In desperate situations, morning dew can be harvested. The yield is pitifully low, but potentially life-saving. You'll need towels (or a good absorbent shammy) and lots of plant life in the immediate area. Wipe the dew off the grass and plant leaves, then ring out the towels into a sanitized container. Make sure the plants you wipe the dew from are not poisonous! You could also put out a large plastic sheet at night and harvest the dew from that first thing in the morning. If the dew is heavy, you could hold the corners of the plastic tarp up and have the dew all run down into the middle and collect there. You might get a couple shot-glasses worth of water that way from a good-sized tarp

Local plant life may provide additional methods of producing small quantities of water. If there are fruit trees around, you can become hydrated by simply eating the fruit – this includes the fruits of the prickly pear and barrel cactus which grow in the wild. That is, by the way, the best way to get water from a cactus by far. The old legend of finding life-saving water in a cactus is mostly only true in cartoons. The only types of cactus which are safe for retrieving water from are the barrel and prickly pear cactus, and they both produce edible (even tasty!) fruit. If these types of cactus are around, just find some that have fruit and eat it. If there is no fruit on them, you can get water from a barrel cactus by scraping out the inside flesh and pressing it, or chewing it to suck the water out then spitting out the flesh. You may need a machete to cut the top of the cactus off first. The same can be done with a prickly pear cactus if you can positively identify the species – but, and this is a big but, prickly pear cactus is very similar in appearance to other forms of cactus which are toxic. The one sure way to identify the species is by the fruit, and if there is fruit, you should just eat that instead, as you will get more fluid from it than from the cactus flesh.

Certain plants have conical leaves or flowers that will capture rainwater in small quantities. Make sure you know the plant is not poisonous before collecting such water.

Finally, plants with thick green fleshy leaves hold water that can be forced to condensate out of it. To accomplish this, you need to create a distilling condition, which is best done in the heat of the day. A pit can be dug in which a bucket is set into, surrounded by thick green fleshy leaf clippings. Stretch a plastic tarp over the pit and seal it the best you can with rocks. The water from within the leaves will evaporate as the day gets hot and collect on the inside of the tarp, then eventually drip down into the bucket. A simpler method of forcing plants to condensate is to just cover them in a plastic trash bag and close the bag around it as tight as you can; there should be a little water gathered in it the bag after the hottest part of the day.

Harvesting H2o

Practical Water Storage Solutions

After securing the renewable resources for your water supply needs, and then arriving at the method of treatment for your drinking water, the next natural step to consider is the storage of your potable water. This is not a huge issue if you have a deep well with a backup pumping solution in place. In that case, you know you can always draw good water from your well, and it's why having a professionally-drilled well is a worthwhile long-term investment. The only thing that could go wrong is an earthquake which destroys your well or moves the water table away, which is a legitimate concern. For that reason, it's a good idea to keep equipment on hand for rainwater collection and shallow well drilling.

Most preppers and homesteaders are interested in storing up an emergency supply of potable water. There is an interesting assortment of water storage containers being sold to this market, but you may be more prone to a do-it-yourself type approach. Either way, you need sanitary, food-grade containers. They fall into four general categories: tanks, barrels, buckets, and jugs.

Tanks

A tank would be anything bigger than you are. You can get them in metal or plastic up to 250 gallons in capacity. Plastic ones have a much shorter shelf life. The Poly-Mart brand makes quality plastic tanks out of polyethylene with a five-year warranty, which is about the longest warranty you will find on this type of product. Some of them are thick enough to ward off freezing temperatures. If stored indoors away from sunlight in a pest-controlled environment, I would expect the actual shelf-life to be at least 2-3 times the warranty. One nice thing about the plastic tanks is they typically hold significantly more water than a similar-sized metal tank. They are also much lighter and easier to move.

The HTP brand of water storage tanks are made from stainless steel and are billed as an add-on to your water heater system. Now we are talking my language. They basically double your hot-water capacity, and boast a heat-loss rate of less than 1 degree Fahrenheit per hour. The problem is that your plumbing draws the water from this extra tank instead of the hot water heater directly, if used as intended. What I would do is simply hook it up to the hot water heater to fill it, then seal it up and reconnect the hot water heater to the plumbing as normal. That would be a very convenient way to fill an extra 45-gallon water storage container. And who says you can only have one? I envision a series of them all rigged together just like a series of rain barrels.

Of course, hot water heaters themselves are good storage tanks all by themselves. Picture a line of five hot water heaters all piped together in a single line. The first one is heated in the normal manner. So is the last. The three in the middle are not. Hot water is taken into your plumbing from the last tank. Get the idea here? The great thing about hot water heaters is they sanitize incoming water (it does need to be clear water on the intake, so if it is fed from a shallow well, I would run it through an inline filter of some kind). The water is drawn through all five tanks and reheated in the last one before being delivered to your sinks and faucets. The fourth tank, second to last in line, will always hold room-temperature, sanitized water. You could use the HTP storage tanks as the three in the middle if you like. In an emergency, you have 200+ gallons of good, freshly sanitized water in a setup like this – but of course, you need room for all the tanks in your plumbing scheme.

Barrels

Water storage barrels are just smaller tanks, typically holding 15-75 gallons each. They are often referred to as drums. All the units I could find for sale in this size range were plastic (polyethylene). This seems like the least convenient way to go if you ask me, as barrels are big enough to be heavy and difficult to move, but must be filled by hand. The coolest barrel setup I have seen was a set of 8 of them being sold by a large warehouse discount store, 55 gallons each. They include bungs, bung wrenches, water pumps, siphon hoses, and water treatment tablets. The brand name is Shelf-Reliance. Don't use the water treatment tablets, however – purify the water you store first in your own chosen manner and just fill the containers with it. This system stores 440 gallons of water.

Buckets

Buckets are smaller than barrels, but there is some crossover here. Let's call buckets containers that hold 3 to 20 gallons. The best source for finding these is homebrew supply stores. Home brewers use food-grade plastic buckets for fermenting their beer in. The most popular size by far is 5-gallons, but you can get them up to 20 gallons in size. The buckets come with airtight lids. You can get both the buckets and the lids with or without holes drilled in them. For water storage, you will want lids with no holes, but you may want the hole at the bottom of the side of the bucket. It can be sealed with a rubber stopper, or you can install the plastic spigot that the brewers use. The spigot is nice when it comes time to dispense the water, but it adds the risk of losing the water through a leak (or the spigot getting opened by the bucket being bumped into something) over long-term storage.

A really cool storage container in the bucket category is known as a *water brick*. These are stackable 3-5 gallon containers that look like the 5-gallon drinking water vessels sold in supermarkets, rectangular in shape with handles. Water bricks stack together, however, snapping into place to use storage space efficiently. They stack sideways as well as on top of each other, to eventually make one very large brick out of however many you choose to stack together. They must be filled manually. One advantage is that you only need to pull out and crack one brick at a time when it comes time to access some of your stored water.

Jugs

This is the real do-it-yourself category. Therefore, we need to talk about sanitizing. If you are reusing jugs that used to contain something other than potable water, they need to be cleaned **and** sanitized. Please note cleaning is not the same thing as sanitizing.

Cleaning should be done with plain old dishwashing soap, hot water, and elbow grease until the vessel appears sparkling clean. Then you need to sanitize it. Theoretically, the hot water from your sink should sanitize it, if the water is hot enough. But plastic containers may have scratches in them where bacteria can hide. Therefore, a cheap sanitizing solution should be used and then rinsed with hot water. Mix one ounce (or one shot glass) of household bleach per five gallons of water for your sanitizing solution, and allow 15 minutes of contact in each plastic vessel. Then rinse them well with hot water.

The moonshiners on television may still use plastic milk cartons, but that is not the best choice for storing potable water because the expected shelf life is only a few years. Much better are plastic PET bottles, which have a very long expected shelf life. If you drink diet soda from these things, save them up and then clean and sanitize both the bottles and the caps before re-using them. Otherwise, you can buy them online brand new (probably from a homebrew supply store).

Canning jars are good for storing water. This is something many doomsday preppers are likely to have on hand already. I would boil the water before adding it to canning jars, just like you do when you are pickling. Screw the lid on the jars after pouring in the boiling water (using an oven mitt) quickly, and it will form an airtight seal that will be just as hard to get off as a pickle jar lid when you want the water. Let the jars cool naturally and slowly; if you subject them to cold water to try to cool them they will break.

Other Interesting Water Gadgets

Let's close the book by looking at a few neat gadgets which didn't quite fit in to any of the other chapters, but may be interesting enough to pursue. If you have any suggestions for additions to this section, please email them to me and I may include them in revised editions, giving you proper credit. You can contact me through my Amazon Author page.

Solar Stills

I briefly suggested a simple version of this in the chapter on *Other Sources of Water in the Wild*, forcing thick plant leaves to condensate by placing them in a hole in the ground around a bucket with a plastic tarp stretched over the top of the hole. If you want to get serious and do this right, the process is known as a making a *solar still*. You don't even need any plant leaves to produce water this way, although adding them will increase your yield somewhat. There is usually enough moisture in the soil alone to create about a pint of water per day (per still) using this method. Solar stills work best when the days are hot but the nights are cold, such as in the southern deserts during sunny winter days.

You need a large sheet of plastic tarp, such as a 12' x 12' painter's drop cloth. You then need to dig a conical-shaped hole that is about 8-9 feet in diameter. A pot or bucket is placed at the very bottom of the hole, preferably mostly buried in its own small hole. The depth of the hole from ground-level to the rim of the bucket should be about two feet.

Now you need to arrange the plastic sheet over the hole so it forms an inverted cone. This can be done by placing a rock in the middle of the sheet, so it sets just above the bucket at the bottom of the hole. You want to have about 6 inches of clearance between the low point of the plastic sheet under the rock and the rim of the bucket. The entire sheet must be suspended above the sides of the hole. Secure the edges of the sheet on the ground outside the hole somehow, perhaps by using bigger rocks. Seal it the best you can to keep the wind from flapping the plastic

During the heat of the day, condensation will form on the underside of the plastic sheet. Because it is angled down toward the center, the beads of newly-formed water will run down and finally collect at the low point, where it will all drip off into the bucket. After a few days, you will have sucked all the moisture out of that hole and will need to dig another one to transfer the tarp to.

Theoretically, this is distilled water that is collected and can be drunk directly. Practically, I would treat the water before consuming it.

Pocket Water Filters

What a day and age we live in. You can purchase lightweight, portable water filters which weigh less than two pounds. These are a great gadget for hikers and campers. They are powered by a built-in hand pump and can output as much as a quart per minute. The filters are fine and include embedded silver particles in them; some also have carbon elements. I have read that the average expected filter life is more than 12,000 gallons. This device can make drinking water from most sources of water in the wild, removing all bacteria, protozoa, and small particles including pollen. They will not remove all viruses, however; therefore, it is best to get the source water from a moving stream or recently deposited rainwater from rock depressions. Two popular manufactures are Katadyn and MSR.

Ultraviolet Water Purifiers

Another type of water purification system uses ultraviolet rays to destroy pathogens. This is, in effect, a radiation treatment. It should be noted that the microorganisms in the water are not removed by this method, just killed – or more accurately stated, deactivated. It is possible for them to reactivate after this treatment, so water purified by UV rays should be consumed quickly. Better yet, filter it after the UV treatment.

Short-wave UV rays are used to treat the water. They do not occur naturally (underneath the atmosphere layer of the earth, anyway) and are produced electronically inside the water-purifier devices. These purifier gadgets are typically cylindrical in shape and come in all different sizes, from huge industrial-sized units to small portable ones that run on battery power. You must have access to electricity to run these, one way or another.

Water goes in one end of the tube, is treated inside with the UV rays, and comes out the other. The flow rate is surprisingly fast, as the water only needs enough treatment time for the light to come into contact with everything in the water. For that reason, however, only reasonably clear water can effectively be treated with ultraviolet rays.

Micro-Purification

There are some purification products being sold which are designed for treating very small batches, such as a single glass of drinking water. One such product that has already been touched upon somewhat is the water purification tablet. This is nothing more than a chlorine or iodine pill which dissolves in water. Make sure you use the proper mix ratio. Given a choice, I would lean toward the chlorine tablets, being as iodine can have harmful long-term health effects. Water purification tablets are not practical for home-water treatment because they are so much more expensive than simply using household bleach (and for storage purposes, the Calcium Hypochlorite granule form is preferred). However, they do come in handy when hiking or travelling in the wild. A canteen can be safely refilled with wild water by first coarse-filtering the water through a cotton shirt or towel, and then purifying the contents of the canteen by dropping in a tablet.

I found a news story on a product now under development in Europe known as the *Nano Tea Bag* water purifier. The press releases do not describe exactly what the scientific process is; only that activated carbon is involved and somehow the bags "suck in" and trap all the impurities. One tea bag can supposedly treat up to one liter of water. This should be an interesting product to watch.

Harvesting H2o

About the Author

Nicholas Hyde is a scholar, researcher, and enthusiastic hobbyist. He writes how-to articles and books on a wide range of topics that interest him, from home brewing to survival techniques (actually he considers home brewing to be a survival technique). His style is one that presents a practical education on the topic at hand, which enables the reader to approach their project with both the knowledge necessary to succeed, and the enthusiasm to enjoy it. Hyde lives in Southern California with his wife and writes when he is not kayak fly-fishing.

Other Books by Nicholas Hyde:

Preparing for Off-Grid Survival*: How to live a self-sufficient, modern-day life off the grid.*

21231667R00057